COLORING BOOK

BY STEPH HALLIGAN

www.ArtToSelf.com

ISBN-13: 978-0692752524
ISBN-10: 0692752528

Test out your materials on this page!

Have fun coloring these cartoons!
Feel free to share your creations with me on Instagram (*@stephaniehalligan*)
and Facebook (*Facebook.com/ArtToSelf*). I'd love to see what you make.

BREATHE

DO WHAT'S NATURAL

IT'S OKAY TO STAND OUT

LET IT BE
AWKWARD

EMBRACE THE
FEAR MONSTER

PLAY WITH YOUR WILD SIDE

FIND THE MAGIC

EXERCISE SOME

SELF LOVE

CELEBRATE THE
SMALL WINS

EMBRACE THE JOMO

(JOY OF MISSING OUT)

LET IT UNFOLD

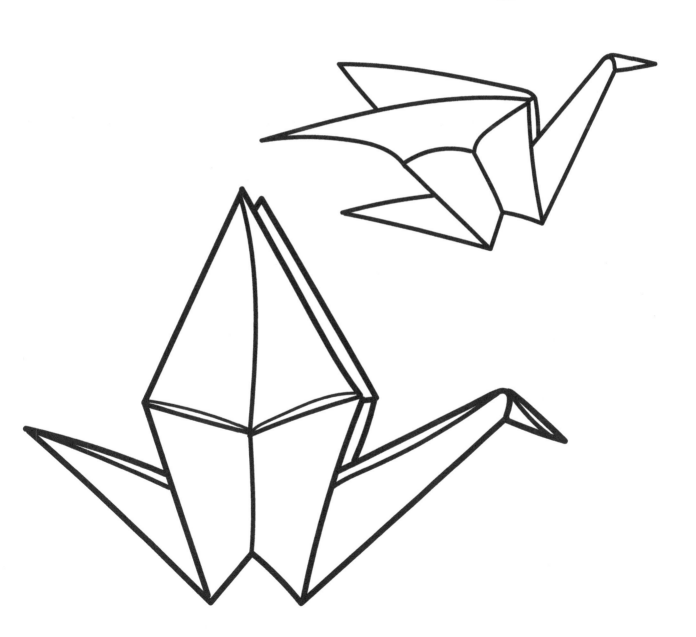

FILL UP YOUR
OWN CUP FIRST

SHINE YOUR LIGHT

TODAY YOU LET IT GO

THERE'S NO
PRESSURE

THE PIECES WILL
COME TOGETHER

THERE'S
MORE
ON THE WAY

 .

FEED YOUR NEEDS

TAKE IT NICE
AND SLOW

LET YOURSELF
RECHARGE

YOU MAKE TIME

JUST MAKE
ONE LITTLE
MOVE

TRUST
YOU HAVE
THE
POWER

BURN BRIGHT
NOT OUT

CHOOSE THE ADVENTURE

DEAR SELF,

This last page is all yours!

ABOUT THE AUTHOR

Steph Halligan is a cartoonist and author living in Boulder, Colorado. She is the author of *Art to Self: Cartoon Notes to Remind You of Your Awesomeness* and *Happy to Be Me, A Tree.*

Her daily inspirational cartoon notes can be found at ArtToSelf.com